POWER
YESTERDAY • TODAY • TOMORROW

ENERGY
FROM
PLANTS AND TRASH

by Ruth Owen

PowerKiDS
press

New York

Published in 2013 by The Rosen Publishing Group, Inc.
29 East 21st Street, New York, NY 10010

Produced for Rosen by Ruby Tuesday Books Ltd
Editor for Ruby Tuesday Books Ltd: Mark J. Sachner
US Editor: Sara Antill
Designer: Emma Randall
Consultant: Dr. Kenneth Leiper, Biofuel Research Centre, Edinburgh Napier University, Edinburgh, Scotland

Photo Credits:
Cover, 2–3, 4–5, 6–7, 9, 10–11, 12–13, 14–15, 16–17, 18–19 (top), 21 (bottom), 22, 23 (top), 26, 27 (bottom), 28–29 © Shutterstock; 17 (top) © US Navy; 18–19 (bottom), 20–21 (top) © FLPA; 23 (bottom), 24–25 © Science Photo Library; 27 (top) © Alamy.

Library of Congress Cataloging-in-Publication Data

Owen, Ruth, 1967–
 Energy from plants and trash : biofuels and biomass power / by Ruth Owen.
    p. cm. — (Power: yesterday, today, tomorrow)
 Includes index.
 ISBN 978-1-4777-0267-3 (library binding) — ISBN 978-1-4777-0273-4 (pbk.) — ISBN 978-1-4777-0274-1 (6-pack)
 1. Biomass energy—Juvenile literature. I. Title.
 TP339.O94 2013
 333.95'39—dc23
                                    2012022550

Manufactured in the United States of America

CPSIA Compliance Information: Batch #W13PK7 For Further Information contact Rosen Publishing, New York, New York at 1-800-237-9932

CONTENTS

Trees, Corn Cobs, Trash, and Elephant Dung

Corn is just one of many crops grown for making biofuels.

What do a forest, a field of corn, a trash can filled with old newspapers and leftovers, and a big pile of elephant dung all have in common?

They are all sources of **biomass** and contain the energy to fuel cars and trucks, heat and light our homes, run our TVs and computers, and power our world.

Biomass is material that comes from living things such as animals and plants. Some types of biomass, such as wood from trees, can be burned to make energy. Others, such as corn, can be turned into liquid **biofuels** to be used in vehicles. Trash and animal dung produce gases that can be used to make electricity.

Worldwide, scientists and engineers are engaged in a race against time to find ways to create energy from biomass. But why do we need to do this when we have gasoline to fill our cars' tanks, and coal and **natural gas** to power our homes, schools, and work places? The answers to that question are simple. The fuels we've relied on for decades are damaging our Earth. What's more, they are running out—fast!

Animal dung is a smelly, but useful, type of biomass!

This forest of trees has been specially grown to be cut down for lumber.

Ancient Biomass Fuels

Oil, gas, and coal, the main fuels we use today, are all made from biomass. They are known as **fossil fuels** because they formed from the remains of animals and plants that died hundreds of millions of years ago.

Most fossil fuels have to be extracted, or removed, from deep underground. Oil is pumped from the ground (on land or under the ocean) as crude oil. At **oil refineries**, crude oil is processed to make gasoline and **diesel**.

Gas is pumped from below the ground and delivered through pipes to homes and businesses, where it is used to power stoves and heating systems.

Much of the coal that is mined is burned in power stations. The coal burns inside huge boilers that heat water to such a high temperature that it becomes steam. Then the steam is used to turn giant **turbines** that generate electricity.

Fossil fuels have powered our world for decades, but now they are running out. These fuels took millions of years to form, and we cannot make more. When they are gone, they are gone!

HOW OIL AND GAS FORMED

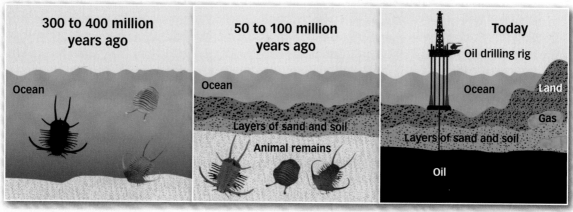

1. Sea plants and animals die and decay on the seabed.

2. Over time, the remains are buried by layers of sand and other soils. Heat and pressure turn them into oil and gas.

3. Today, we extract oil and gas from under the ground.

HOW COAL FORMED

300 to 400 million years ago	50 to 100 million years ago	Today

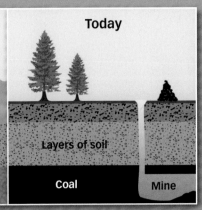

Ocean

Layers of soil

Dead Plants

Layers of soil

Coal

Mine

1. Plants die and settle on the bottoms of swamps, where they decay.

2. Over millions of years, the plant remains are covered by layers of soil and water.

3. Heat and pressure turn the plant remains into coal. Today, we mine the coal from underground.

Deep underground in a coal mine, a coal miner drills into a wall of coal.

An oil rig extracts oil from the ground beneath the ocean.

FAST FACT

*Earth's **natural resources**, such as oil, coal, or plants, can be grouped as being **renewable** or **nonrenewable**. It's possible to grow more plants, so they are called renewable resources. Fossil fuels, such as coal and oil, however, are nonrenewable because we cannot produce more of them.*

Fuel and Our Changing Climate

Even if we could create more fossil fuels, the fact is it wouldn't be a good idea. Our use of fossil fuels is harming our planet by causing a gradual increase in Earth's temperatures, which is known as **climate change**.

Most scientists agree that climate change is happening because of our use of fossil fuels. When we burn oil in vehicles or coal in an electricity power plant, gases such as carbon dioxide, methane, and nitrous oxide are released into the Earth's **atmosphere**. These gases are known as **greenhouse gases** because they trap the Sun's heat on Earth in the way that a greenhouse traps heat inside. We need heat and light from the Sun in order to survive. Too much heat, however, is a big problem.

Warmer temperatures will cause ocean levels to rise because water expands when it is heated. Also, glaciers and the giant ice caps at the North and South poles could melt and flow into the oceans. Higher sea levels will mean low-lying coastal places, such as London and New York City, could disappear under water!

FAST FACT

While some parts of the world flood, climate change will make others so hot and dry that people will have trouble growing food. Lakes and rivers will dry up, making it hard for people and animals to find enough water.

In today's world, our use of vehicles and electricity adds greenhouse gases to Earth's atmosphere day and night.

Biomass Power

Today, most people agree that we need to be using fuels that are renewable and make fewer greenhouse gases than fossil fuels. Energy made from biomass is one solution. So what types of biomass fuel are available?

Bioethanol: Running Cars on Plants

Bioethanol is a fuel that can be mixed with regular gasoline or used on its own in cars designed to run on biofuel. Bioethanol can be made from plants such as corn, wheat, and sugar cane.

Biodiesel: Trucks Fueled by Soybeans

Most trucks, buses, and tractors run on diesel, which is made from crude oil. These vehicles could be run on biodiesel, a fuel made from soybeans, oil palm tree fruit and seeds, and other plants that contain a lot of oil. Biodiesel can even be made from used cooking oil.

Corn for making bioethanol is harvested on a farm.

Electricity from Trash

Biomass garbage such as paper, cardboard, food scraps, and lawn clippings can be burned in waste-to-energy power plants to generate electricity.

Biogas: Power from Garbage and Manure

When garbage rots in underground **landfill sites**, it gives off gases, known as **biogas**, which can be collected and burned to generate electricity. Biogas produced by animal manure on farms can be burned to generate electricity.

A bear forages for food on a landfill site.

FAST FACT

In 1960, an average American threw away 2.7 pounds (1.2 kg) of trash each day. Today, that amount has risen to 4.4 pounds (2 kg). Garbage is a big problem that's here to stay. Burning it in waste-to-energy plants disposes of the trash and turns it into a renewable fuel.

Soybeans are grown so that their oil can be extracted and used as cooking oil and in biodiesel.

Bioethanol: Plant Power

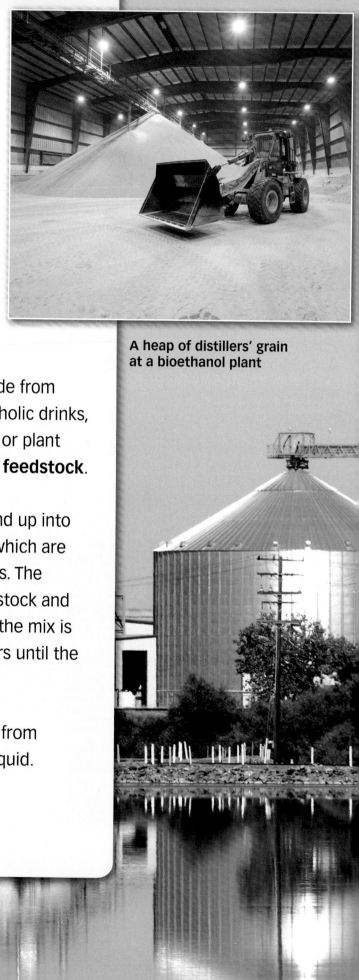

When you see a field of corn you might imagine the tasty food smothered in butter or grilling on a barbecue. The corn, however, may be destined to end up as bioethanol in the fuel tank of a car.

A heap of distillers' grain at a bioethanol plant

Bioethanol is a clear, alcohol fuel that is made from plants in pretty much the same way as alcoholic drinks, such as vodka and gin, are made. The grain, or plant material, used to make the fuel is known as **feedstock**.

At a bioethanol plant, the feedstock is ground up into flour then mixed with water and enzymes, which are chemicals that can cause chemical reactions. The enzymes break down the starch in the feedstock and turn it into sugars. Yeast is then added, and the mix is allowed to sit and ferment for about 50 hours until the sugars become alcohol, or ethanol.

Finally, the ethanol is distilled, or separated, from the solid material in the mix so it is a pure liquid. Then it is ready to be used as fuel.

The plants used to make biofuels are known as feedstock. Many different plants are suitable as feedstock for making bioethanol.

Rice

Sugar cane

Potato skins

Wheat

Barley

Sugar beet

250
≈
250
200
100

A flask of bioethanol

A bioethanol plant

FAST FACT

After the ethanol has been distilled, the solid grain leftovers are dried and then used as feed for farm animals. This feed is known as distillers' grain.

Biodiesel: Do You Smell French Fries?

In the future, the bus you take to school might be running on soybean fuel or have a fuel tank filled with sunflower power!

Vehicles such as buses, trucks, tractors, and taxis usually run on diesel fuel that is made from crude oil. Like fuel for cars, though, diesel can be made from plants. Biodiesel is made from oil extracted from the seeds of oil-rich plants.

The plants used to make biodiesel are renewable, and biodiesel releases fewer greenhouse gases when it burns than diesel made from crude oil.

It's also possible to run diesel vehicles on recycled cooking oil. When a restaurant has finished cooking hundreds of portions of french fries in its deep fat fryer, it has to dispose of the dirty, used oil. Usually, this oil ends up in the ground in a landfill. It can, however, be collected from the restaurant and recycled to power trucks, buses, and taxis. What's more, a vehicle run on used cooking oil will have exhaust fumes that smell of french fries!

Many vehicles on the road today can change to using biodiesel without needing to make changes to their engines.

A field of soybean plants and ripe seeds in a pod

The oil that cooks french fries can be reused to power a diesel vehicle.

FAST FACT

Sunflowers are grown so that the oil from their seeds can be used for cooking. This oil can also be used as biodiesel. When the seeds have been crushed to extract their oil, the leftover material can be used as animal feed.

Could Biofuels Mean Zero Carbon Dioxide?

Bioethanol and biodiesel are both renewable fuels that will not run out like fossil fuels. But how do they shape up when it comes to reducing the amount of greenhouse gases that are released by vehicles?

Vehicles powered by biofuels still release carbon dioxide and other greenhouse gases into the atmosphere. The upside to these fuels, however, is that the plants that are grown to make the fuel will take carbon dioxide back out of the air as they grow!

Plants take in carbon dioxide from the air through tiny holes in their leaves called stomata. Inside their leaves, they use the carbon dioxide, water, and sunlight to make sugars, which they use for energy and growth. This process is called photosynthesis.

Many scientists believe it should be possible for feedstock plants to absorb as much carbon dioxide from the air during photosynthesis as they will release when they are finally burned as fuel! Reducing the amount of this greenhouse gas in the atmosphere will help in the fight against climate change.

Biofuel crops, such as this field of corn, will reduce the amount of carbon dioxide in the atmosphere.

This is the US Navy Green Hornet supersonic jet. Even planes that can fly faster than the speed of sound can be powered by plants!

The Perfect Fuel?

Biofuels are made from a renewable source and they will add less carbon dioxide to the atmosphere than gasoline and regular diesel. It seems as if they must be the perfect vehicle fuel for the future, but are they?

Here are just some of the issues that need to be taken into account when planning a future in which we travel on biofuels.

A field of sunflowers grown for their oil will provide a home for birds, insects, and other animals.

Biofuels Pros

✓ *Not all countries can produce enough crude oil to fulfill their needs. They rely on other countries selling them oil, which then has to be transported creating more greenhouse gases. If they switched to using biofuels, these countries could grow and produce their own fuel.*

✓ *75% of the world's poorest people rely on farming to make their livings. Growing biofuels could be a way for these farmers to earn more money.*

✓ *A lot of land is needed to grow feed crops for the animals that supply us with milk, meat, and eggs. Biofuel crops produce a by-product of animal feed so the amount of land needed for feed crops will be reduced.*

✓ *The United States and Europe grow far more food than is needed, and then sell it cheaply to developing countries. Farmers in these countries can't compete with the imported food. If farmers in wealthier countries grow biofuel crops instead, farmers in poor countries will have the chance to supply their own country's food needs.*

Biofuels Cons

X *Producing fuel is big business. Many people are afraid that more and more wild habitat, such as rain forests in South America and Southeast Asia, will be destroyed to create land for growing biofuel crops.*

X *In order to grow biofuel crops, **fertilizers** (to feed the plants extra nutrients) and pesticides (to kill weeds and insects that eat the crops) have to be manufactured, which uses lots of energy.*

X *Some people are concerned that biofuel crops will be grown on land that is needed for growing food for people.*

X *Plant fertilizers containing nitrogen release the greenhouse gas nitrous oxide into the atmosphere. A quantity of nitrous oxide is 300 times more harmful than the same quantity of carbon dioxide.*

A vast area of Amazon rain forest cleared for growing oil palm plants destroys the home of many birds, insects, and other animals.

Future Biofuels

Today's biofuels are made using only the grain, or seeds, from a plant. The plant's leaves and stems are wasted. Scientists are studying how to make biofuels that use every part of a plant.

The fuel would be made from the cellulose in plants. Cellulose is the material that makes up the walls of a plant's **cells**. Making fuel from cellulose is more complicated than from plant sugars. Once scientists have perfected the process, however, many more feedstocks will become available.

Fuel could be made from specially-planted, fast-growing trees, grasses, and wood scraps as well as sawdust from the lumber industry. It could also be made from straw (stalks and leaves), the left over material when crops such as wheat are harvested for food.

Trees and grasses need less water and fertilizers to grow than crops like corn. These tough plants are also more resistant to insect pests and plant diseases. Like the grass on a lawn, grass crops can be cut, or harvested, more than once in a year, and they do not need to be replanted.

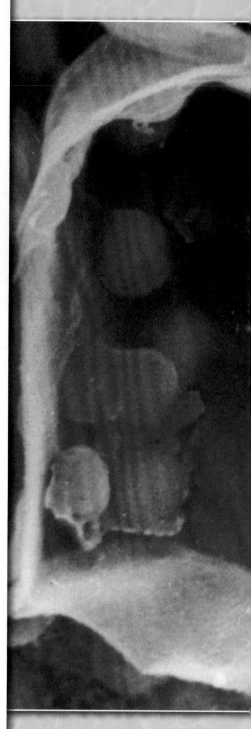

This scanning electron microscope image shows a plant cell close-up.

Cell walls

Switchgrass

FAST FACT

*Switchgrass is a tough, fast-growing prairie grass that could be used for making biofuel. Switchgrass can be grown on dry plains, in swamps, and on the sides of highways. It will survive flooding and live without much water in times of **drought**.*

Algae: The Greenest Green Fuel?

Covering over 70 percent of Earth's surface, water could hold the answer to the problem of where to grow biofuel feedstock.

Water is home to many living things, including algae. Algae are not plants, but a large group of organisms that can be as complex as seaweeds and as simple as green, foamy sludge! Algae contain oil that can be harvested and used as a feedstock for making biofuels. And all algae need to grow is water and sunlight.

Algae can be grown in saltwater, freshwater, and even in wastewater or sewage.

A frog swims through a freshwater pond covered with a layer of algae.

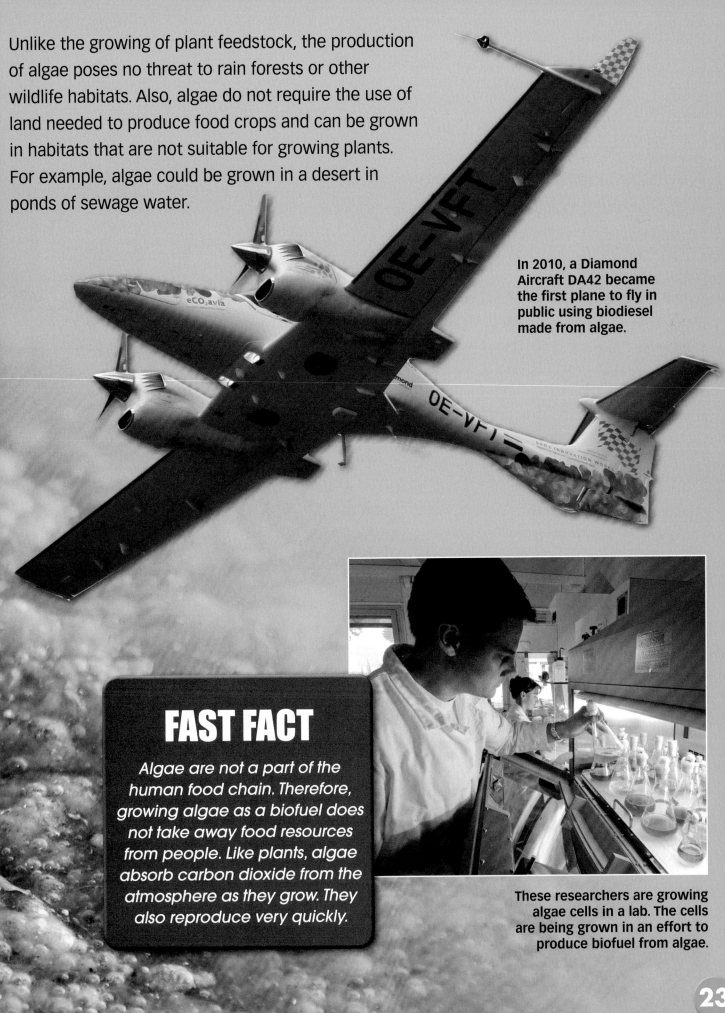

Unlike the growing of plant feedstock, the production of algae poses no threat to rain forests or other wildlife habitats. Also, algae do not require the use of land needed to produce food crops and can be grown in habitats that are not suitable for growing plants. For example, algae could be grown in a desert in ponds of sewage water.

In 2010, a Diamond Aircraft DA42 became the first plane to fly in public using biodiesel made from algae.

FAST FACT

Algae are not a part of the human food chain. Therefore, growing algae as a biofuel does not take away food resources from people. Like plants, algae absorb carbon dioxide from the atmosphere as they grow. They also reproduce very quickly.

These researchers are growing algae cells in a lab. The cells are being grown in an effort to produce biofuel from algae.

Waste-to-Energy

We produce a vast quantity of garbage in our homes that has to be disposed of. We need electricity to power our houses. Put these two needs together, and you get waste-to-energy plants.

About 85 percent of the garbage produced in US homes can be burned, or combusted. Of that combustible rubbish, about 62 percent is biomass such as paper, cardboard, wood, waste food, and yard clippings.

At waste-to-energy plants garbage is used as a fuel instead of the coal used in traditional power plants. The garbage-powered fires boil water to create steam, which then turns turbines that generate electricity. Burning garbage in this way not only produces renewable power, but it also reduces the amount of trash that has to be buried in landfills.

A waste-to-energy plant burning 350,000 tons (318,000 t) of garbage in a year will produce enough electricity to power 20,000 homes during that time.

FAST FACT

Burning garbage produces lots of ash. Huge magnets are used to pull any pieces of metal from the ash. This metal can then be recycled. The ash can be used for building roads and for making blocks for use in construction.

This is the waste pit at a waste-to-energy plant in Connecticut. Each day 2,500 tons (2,268 t) of garbage are delivered by truck to the pit, ready for burning.

Biogas Power

When garbage rots in landfills it releases gases, known as biogas, which are about 60 percent methane. Methane can be harmful to the environment, but it can be used to produce power.

Methane is collected from landfill sites and burned in power plants to create electricity. It can also be used as a fuel for vehicles that have engines adapted to run on biogas.

On a smaller scale, some farmers produce biogas from farm waste. They put manure and plant material into large tanks called biodigesters. As **bacteria** break down this material, methane is released that can be collected and used to make heat and electricity for the farm. If the manure is left to rot outside, the methane will escape into the air.

Collecting methane and using it as a fuel reduces the amount of this greenhouse gas going into the atmosphere. The sources of methane, such as garbage and animal waste, are plentiful, so biogas fuel is renewable. Using biogas instead of burning fossil fuels cuts down on the amount of greenhouse gases released into the atmosphere.

FAST FACT

At the Toronto Zoo, in Canada, manure from elephants, giraffes, and other animals will be used to produce the zoo's electricity and heat. Manure, animal bedding, and food waste from the zoo's restaurants will be turned into biogas fuel in a biodigester.

An elephant at the Toronto Zoo

Each year, this biodigester on a UK farm turns animal and plant waste into enough electricity to power 2,000 houses.

In a day, a cow can produce enough manure to generate sufficient electricity to power a 100-watt light bulb for a day!

Fuel for the Future

Energy such as electricity, gas, and vehicle fuel is essential to our modern lives. We must produce the energy we need, however, in ways that are **sustainable** and will help combat climate change.

Switching to bioethanol and biodiesel fuels and using electricity made from renewable sources is a good start. Developing new biofuels made from plant cellulose or algae will make our energy use even greener.

There are still lots of issues surrounding the production of biofuels, however, because they can be produced in good ways or in bad ways. For example, driving a vehicle that runs on biofuel is a positive step toward helping the planet. If a rain forest was destroyed to produce that fuel, however, the effect is less positive.

Our amazing planet gave us oil, natural gas, and coal, but we didn't use these fossil fuels wisely. Fueling our world with biomass in the future is a huge step toward fixing the damage that's been done. It's important for everyone on Earth that we get it right this time!

A crop of renewable, sustainable canola, which is used to produce biodiesel.

FAST FACT

While scientists work to find environmentally-friendly solutions for our future energy needs, we can help out by saving energy. Driving less, switching off lights, TVs, and computers, and reusing and recycling instead of creating trash, are all ways we can reduce our energy usage.

Glossary

atmosphere (AT-muh-sfeer)
The layer of gases surrounding a planet, moon, or star.

bacteria (bak-TIR-ee-uh)
Tiny living things that can only be seen using a microscope. Some bacteria are helpful, for example, breaking down waste products, while others can cause diseases.

biofuels (by-oh-FYOO-elz)
Fuels made from biomass such as plants.

biogas (BY-oh-gas)
A gas produced when biomass, such as plant material or animal manure, decomposes, or rots.

biomass (BY-oh-mas)
A renewable energy source that has come from living things such as animals and plants.

cell (SEL)
The smallest unit of life that may be called a living thing. All life forms are made of cells.

climate change (KLY-mut CHAYNJ)
The gradual warming of temperatures on Earth.

diesel (DEE-zel)
A fuel made from oil that is used by trucks, buses, and other vehicles with diesel engines.

drought (DROWT)
A period of lower than normal rainfall, which causes water supplies in an area to dry up.

feedstock (FEED-stok)
The raw material from which a product, such as bioethanol, is produced.

fertilizer (FUR-tuh-lyz-er)
Chemicals or natural materials, such as manure, used to feed plants.

fossil fuels (FO-sul FYOOLZ)
Fuels that formed over millions of years from the remains of plants and animals. Oil, natural gas, and coal are all fossil fuels.

greenhouse gases
(GREEN-hows GAS-ez)
Gases such as carbon dioxide, methane, and nitrous oxide that are released into Earth's atmosphere when fossil fuels are burned.

landfill site (LAND-fil SYT)
A large hole in the ground where garbage is buried.

natural gas (NA-chuh-rul GAS)
A fossil fuel that formed underground over millions of years. It is piped to homes and businesses to be used as a source of energy.

nonrenewable (non-ree-NOO-uh-bul)
A resource, such as coal, that cannot be renewed once it is used.

oil refinery (OY-ul rih-FY-neh-ree)
A plant where crude oil is processed to make gasoline, diesel, and to be used in products such as plastics and makeup.

renewable (ree-NOO-uh-bul)
A resource, such as plants, that can be produced again and again and will not run out.

sustainable (suh-STAY-nuh-bel)
Using resources in a way that can continue into the future without causing damage to the environment.

turbine (TER-byn)
A machine with a wheel or rotor that turns and generates power. A turbine can be driven by gas, water, or steam.

WEBSITES

Due to the changing nature of Internet links, PowerKids Press has developed an online list of websites related to the subject of this book. This site is updated regularly. Please use this link to access the list:

www.powerkidslinks.com/pytt/bio/

Read More

Solway, Andrew. *Biofuels.* Energy for the Future and Global Warming. New York: Gareth Stevens, 2008.

Spilsbury, Richard, and Louise Spilsbury. *Fossil Fuel Power.* Let's Discuss Energy Resources. New York: PowerKids Press, 2012.

Weakland, Mark. *Onion Juice, Poop, and Other Surprising Sources of Alternative Energy.* Nasty (But Useful!) Science. Mankato, MN: Capstone Press, 2009.

Index